Boys Just Like Me

Like Me

BIBLE MEN WHO TRUSTED GOD

Copyright © Jean Stapleton 2017
ISBN: 978-1-78191-998-9
10 9 8 7 6 5 4 3 2 1

Published by Christian Focus Publications Ltd,
Geanies House, Fearn, Tain, Ross-shire,
IV20 1TW, Scotland, U.K.
Tel: 01862 871011
Fax: 01862 871699
www.christianfocus.com
email: info@christianfocus.com

Cover design by Tom Barnard
Cover and inside illustrations by Jeff Anderson
Printed and bound in China

Boys Just Like Me

BIBLE MEN WHO TRUSTED GOD

Jean Stapleton

CF4•K

CONTENTS

Just Like Me

**'Elijah was a man with a nature
like ours...' James 5:17**

In the Bible we read about men and women who God chose for some special work. Elijah was a prophet: God spoke to Elijah so that he could tell the people what God wanted them to know. God also helped Elijah to do wonderful things, so that the people would know that the words he spoke really were from God. We will learn more about Elijah further on in this book.

We might think that people like Elijah were different from us, much braver than we are. But our verse today teaches us that Elijah was like us. He could feel afraid or tired or lonely like we do. Elijah trusted God and obeyed God. He believed that God would give him strength to do the things He asked him to do.

In this book we will learn about other men who trusted God like Elijah did. There is much

more to read in the Bible about these men. I hope that you will soon be able to read more for yourself.

PRAY: That God will help you to learn something each day about what it means to trust Him.

DAY 1

Abel Does Right
Read: Genesis 4:3-5

Adam and Eve were the first people that God created. They had two sons whose names were Cain and Abel.

God had made a perfect world. He gave Adam and Eve just one rule to keep. However, they disobeyed Him. That was how sin came into the world. Everyone born into the world since then, except the Lord Jesus, is sinful. We all do, say and think things that are wrong.

God promised to send someone to save us from our sin. We now know that this is Jesus, who died to take sin's punishment for everyone who trusts in Him.

In Old Testament days, an animal died instead of the person who had sinned: we call this a sacrifice. It would not take away the person's sin. It showed that they were very sorry for their sin. They were trusting in God to send the promised Saviour. It was like a picture of what He would do.

Cain and Abel knew about sacrifices. One day Cain brought some of the food he had grown, as an offering to God. Abel brought one of his sheep as a sacrifice. God was satisfied with what Abel did. It showed that Abel understood that the animal died instead of him, so that his sin could be forgiven.

Cain knew that God was not pleased with him or with the offering he brought. Instead of putting things right, he was angry with his brother. He did a terrible thing. When the two brothers were out in the field, Cain killed his brother Abel.

Abel had done what was right. We read in the New Testament that Abel offered the right sacrifice because he trusted in God ('by faith' – Hebrews chapter 11 verse 4)

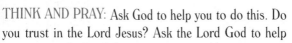

THINK AND PRAY: Ask God to help you to do this. Do you trust in the Lord Jesus? Ask the Lord God to help you trust in the Lord Jesus.

DAY 2

Noah Obeys God
Read: Genesis 6:5 and 8

Have you seen pictures of flooding when rivers overflow? Water may cover roads and fields, and sometimes gets into people's homes.

Long ago, when Noah was alive no-one had ever seen a large flood. God told Noah that because the people were so wicked, He was going to send a flood. He told him to build an ark, like a large wooden boat. God gave Noah all the instructions he would need. He told him what sort of wood to use and how big to make the ark.

God is patient. He gave the people a long time to be sorry for their wicked ways. The people did not love God or want to please Him. They did not believe that God would punish them for their sin.

Noah believed God and he did what God had told him to do. It must have taken a long time to build the ark, which was about 140 metres long.

The ark had to be very big because God had said there must be some of every kind of animal and bird in the ark. There must be seven of some sorts of animals and two of other sorts. There would need to be plenty of room to store food for all the animals.

Seven days before the rain began, God told Noah that he and his family must go into the ark. Noah and his wife, and Noah's sons Ham, Shem and Japheth and their wives did as God said. You may wonder how Noah managed to bring all the animals into the ark. Just as God had promised, once Noah was in the ark, the animals came to him. (Genesis chapter 6 verse 20 and chapter 7 verses 8 and 9.)

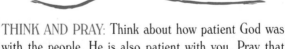

THINK AND PRAY: Think about how patient God was with the people. He is also patient with you. Pray that God will help you to believe what He says in the Bible. Ask Him to help you to do what He says, whatever other people do.

11

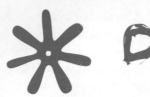

DAY 3

Noah is Safe
Read: Genesis 7:1-5

Once Noah and his family, and all the animals were in the ark, God shut the door. This was important: Noah and his family would be safe because it was God who shut them in. The other people were shut out. Only God knew when they had had long enough to be sorry for their sin. All the time Noah was building the ark, he had warned the people about what was going to happen. No-one except his own family, had listened to Noah. Only eight people were safe in the ark.

It rained for forty days and forty nights. The whole earth was flooded. Even the mountains were covered with water. Only the eight people in the ark and the animals with them, were saved from drowning. They lived in the ark for just over a year. When the water had gone down and the ground was dry, God told Noah that it was time to leave the ark.

We can learn from the ark that there was one way to safety: one door. The Lord Jesus said that He is the one way to God. We have sinful hearts and so we do things that are wrong. Our sin stops us knowing God as our Friend. The Lord Jesus died on the cross to take the punishment for the sin of everyone who trusts in Him.

THINK AND PRAY: Noah believed what God said. He trusted God to keep him safe in the ark. God has told us in the Bible that everyone who trusts in the Lord Jesus will be forgiven for all the wrong things they have done. They will be kept safe with God for ever. When you pray today, say thank you to God for the Bible. In the Bible God teaches us how He takes care of everyone who trusts in Him.

DAY 4

Abram lived about two thousand years before the Lord Jesus was born in Bethlehem. He lived in a city called Ur in the land we now call Iraq. But the people of Ur did not love God, they bowed down to idols. Idols are false gods, like statues made out of wood or stone, gold or silver. They may look like people or animals, or even like the sun or the moon.

God told Abram to leave Ur and the people that he knew there. Abram did not know where God wanted him to live. But God made a promise. A great nation – many people – would come from his family. From Abram's family good would come to families all over the world.

When a family moves house, they have usually chosen the house they will live in. It was not like that for Abram and Sarai his wife. Abram did not know where God wanted him to live. Abram obeyed God. He travelled with his father, his wife and his nephew Lot, to a place called Haran.

While they were in Haran, Abram's father died. Abram knew that he had further to travel. He was seventy-five years old and Sarai was sixty-five years old when they set out once again. This time they came into the land of Canaan. Then God spoke to Abram another time. He told him that this was the land he would give to his family. Abram did not have a comfortable house in Canaan like he probably had in Ur. He and his wife lived in tents and sometimes moved to different parts of the land.

THINK AND PRAY: Abram showed that he trusted God, by doing what God asked him to do. Ask God to help you trust in Him and obey Him.

DAY 5

Abraham's Family Tree
Read: Genesis 21:3;
Matthew 1:1-2 and 16

God had promised Abram that many people would come from his family. Abram believed God's promises even though it was twenty-five years before his son Isaac was born.

In Genesis chapter 17 we read that God changed Abram's name to Abraham. The name Abraham means 'father of a multitude' (many people). Sarai's name was changed to Sarah (princess).

As the years went by, Abraham's family grew very large. His grandson Jacob had twelve sons. They all grew up and had families of their own. These families became the twelve tribes of Israel.

Do you remember something about families in God's promise to Abraham? We read in Genesis chapter 12 verse 3 that good would come to families all over the world through Abraham's family ('all the families of the earth shall be blessed'). These words are about the coming of the Lord Jesus.

A family tree is not a tree that grows in the garden. It is a list of the names of people belonging to a family. It shows how the family has grown. We find Abraham's family tree in Matthew chapter 1. This family tree is a long one. There were about two thousand years between Abraham in verse 1 and the Lord Jesus in verse 16.

Abraham believed God's promises even when it was hard to see how what God promised could happen. When Isaac was born, Abraham and Sarah were much older than people usually are when a baby is born. While they waited many years for their son to be born, God was teaching them to trust Him.

THINK AND PRAY: As we read about Abraham's story in the Bible, we are also learning that God always does what He says he will do. When you pray thank God that we can trust Him just as Abraham did long ago.

DAY 6

Isaac Brings Joy
Read: Genesis 24:3-4

The name Isaac means laughter. Isaac brought a lot of joy to Abraham and Sarah. They had waited so long for the son God had promised them.

When Isaac grew up, Abraham knew that it was very important that he had the right wife. The people in Canaan worshipped idols. Abraham sent his most trusted servant to the city of Haran, where his relations lived. He told his servant he must bring a wife for Isaac from there.

It was a long journey to Haran. God helped Abraham's servant to meet Rebekah who was the granddaughter of Abraham's brother. Rebekah was willing to go with the servant. Isaac and Rebekah were married and the Bible tells us that Isaac loved Rebekah.

For a long time Isaac and Rebekah had no children. Isaac knew about God's promise to the family of Abraham. He prayed that Rebekah would have a baby.

God heard Isaac's prayer. Rebekah had twin boys, named Jacob and Esau. As they grew up, they were very different. Esau liked to be out hunting in the fields. Jacob cared more about his family and especially about God's promise to them.

Although Jacob and Esau were twins, Esau was counted as the oldest because he was born first. Esau would expect to be the head of the family when Isaac died. But before the twins were born, God had told Rebekah that the second twin would be the head of the family.

Rebekah was afraid that Isaac would give his blessing to Esau. This would make him the head of the family. Isaac was by now very old and could not see very well. Rebekah persuaded Jacob to pretend to be Esau. This way, she made sure that Jacob would be the family head, as God had told her years before.

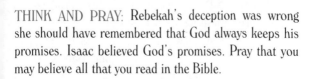

THINK AND PRAY: Rebekah's deception was wrong she should have remembered that God always keeps his promises. Isaac believed God's promises. Pray that you may believe all that you read in the Bible.

DAY 7

Jacob Travels Home
Read: Genesis 28:15-16

Esau was very angry with Jacob. He was so angry, that Isaac and Rebekah decided that Jacob would have to go away. They told him that it would be best for him to go to his uncle Laban's family in Haran.

Jacob set out on the long journey. He rested at night using a stone for a pillow. He had a wonderful dream. He saw a ladder reaching from earth to heaven. Angels were going up and down the ladder. God spoke to Jacob that night.

God gave to Jacob the promises he had made to Abraham about his family. As you read in today's Bible reading, God promised to be with Jacob wherever he went. He also promised to bring him back to that land.

When Jacob awoke, he named the place where God had spoken to him 'Bethel', which means 'House of God'.

Jacob stayed in Haran for twenty years. While he was there he married and had a large family of eleven boys and one girl. He worked hard for Laban, looking after his animals. As the years went by, he had many animals of his own: sheep, goats, cows, camels and donkeys.

After twenty years in Haran, God told Jacob that it was time for him to return to Canaan. Jacob set off with his family, the servants who worked for him, and all his animals.

As Jacob travelled towards Canaan, he thought about his brother. Was Esau still angry with him? He had a message that Esau was coming to meet him with four hundred men.

Jacob was afraid that Esau planned to attack him. He divided his family and his animals into two groups. He thought that if Esau attacked one group, the other group could escape. Then Jacob did what we should always do when we are afraid: he prayed.

THINK AND PRAY: Do you ever feel scared and worried? What is the best thing to do in those situations? Remember that you can talk to God about your problems or whenever you are lonely or afraid.

23

Jacob Meets Esau
Read: Genesis 32:9-12

Today's verses tell us how Jacob prayed. First of all he thought about God, and how it was God who had told him to come back to Canaan. Then he thought about how good God had been to him while he lived in Haran. Jacob did not pretend to be brave. He told God that he was afraid of his brother and asked God to help him.

After he had prayed, he sent presents to Esau. He sent many sheep and goats, camels, cows and donkeys. He thought that when Esau saw what he had sent him, he would stop being angry with him. Jacob then sent his family and all that he had across the River Jabbock. Jacob stayed on his own that night. He knew this was an important time. He was returning to the land that God had promised to his grandfather Abraham's family. God spoke to Jacob that night and gave him a new name: Israel. That name means 'Prince with God'.

The next morning, Jacob crossed the river. He saw Esau and all his men coming towards him. Jacob went ahead of his family and bowed to his brother. This was the moment he had been so afraid of, but God had heard his prayer. Esau ran to meet Jacob and gave him a real brotherly hug. After this, Esau met all of Jacob's family.

At last Jacob was able to settle down in the land of Canaan. He had a twelfth son who was called Benjamin. He and his family lived in tents and sometimes moved to different parts of the land, as Abraham had done.

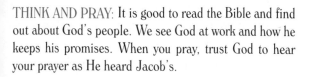

THINK AND PRAY: It is good to read the Bible and find out about God's people. We see God at work and how he keeps his promises. When you pray, trust God to hear your prayer as He heard Jacob's.

DAY 9

Joseph Goes to Egypt
Read: Genesis 41:39-41

Joseph was Jacob's eleventh son, so he had ten older brothers and one younger. His older brothers were all jealous of him because Jacob showed more love to Joseph than to them.

Some very bad things happened to Joseph. One day his brothers put him down a deep pit in the ground where he could not escape. Then they sold him for money to some men travelling to Egypt. Joseph was then sold to an Egyptian man called Potiphar. This meant that he was Potiphar's slave and had to do everything that Potiphar told him to do.

God helped Joseph and everything he did went well. But Potiphar's wife told lies about him and he was put in prison. Even in prison God was with Joseph. The man in charge let Joseph look after the other prisoners.

One day Joseph's life was changed. The King of Egypt, who was called the Pharaoh, sent for him. He had had strange dreams and he had been told that Joseph could understand what dreams meant.

God helped Joseph to understand, and he was able to tell Pharaoh what his dreams meant. Pharaoh's dreams were a warning from God. Egypt would have seven years with plenty of food and then seven years of famine. Famine means that there is no food because the crops have not grown properly.

Joseph was chosen to make sure lots of food was saved in the good years. He would then sell food to the people when the famine came. Joseph would be the most important man in Egypt after Pharaoh.

A lot of bad things had happened to Joseph but he still trusted in God.

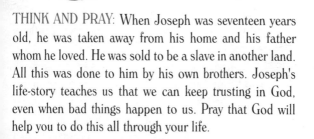

THINK AND PRAY: When Joseph was seventeen years old, he was taken away from his home and his father whom he loved. He was sold to be a slave in another land. All this was done to him by his own brothers. Joseph's life-story teaches us that we can keep trusting in God, even when bad things happen to us. Pray that God will help you to do this all through your life.

DAY 10

Joseph's Brothers Buy Food
Read: Genesis 42:7-8

The famine you read about yesterday spread to other countries. In the land of Canaan, Jacob heard that people could buy food in Egypt. He sent Joseph's ten older brothers to Egypt but kept Benjamin at home.

Joseph saw his brothers when they came to him to buy food. They did not recognise him, but told him about their father and their younger brother in Canaan. Joseph said they must bring Benjamin with them if they came again. One brother, Simeon, was kept in prison in Egypt. Joseph wanted to be sure that his brothers came back.

Joseph's brothers did not want to go back to Egypt. But when there was no more grain left to make bread, Jacob told them that they must go and buy more. Jacob did not want to send Benjamin with them. One of the brothers, called

Judah, said he would look after Benjamin and bring him safely home.

This time Joseph treated his brothers kindly. He arranged for a good meal to be prepared for them. They still did not know that this important man was their brother Joseph. It was at least twenty years since they had been so cruel to him. Joseph had a plan to find out if his brothers were truly sorry for what they had done.

Joseph had his own silver cup put in Benjamin's sack of grain. This made it seem as if Benjamin had stolen it. Joseph said that Benjamin must stay in Egypt.

Judah remembered his promise to his father. He asked if he could stay and work for Joseph instead of Benjamin. Now Joseph was sure that his brothers had changed. They would not treat Benjamin as they had treated him all those years ago.

THINK AND PRAY: We have not all been as cruel as Joseph's brothers were, but we all do wrong things. God has told us about things we should not do, like telling lies or hurting other people. What does God want us to do instead? Pray that God will forgive you for the wrong things you have done.

DAY 11

Jacob Sees Joseph Again
Read: Genesis 50:20-21

At last Joseph was sure that his brothers were no longer as cruel as they had been. They were sorry for what they had done. He sent everyone away except his brothers. Then he told them who he was. They were very frightened. Joseph was now a very important man. Was he going to punish them?

Joseph spoke kindly to his brothers. He told them that it was God who had sent him to Egypt. God knew that Joseph would be able to save the lives of his family when the famine came.

It was two years after the famine started, that Joseph told his brothers who he was. He knew that there would be five more years of famine. Joseph said that his brothers must bring their father, their wives and their children to Egypt.

Pharaoh heard about Joseph's family. He said that he would give them land in Egypt where they could live. He told Joseph to send his brothers home with carts to bring their families in. Joseph did this and also gave them everything they would need for the journey.

At first Jacob could not believe the news. For such a long time he had thought that Joseph had been killed by a wild animal. Now his sons were telling him that Joseph was alive and lived in Egypt. Then Jacob saw the carts that Joseph had sent. It must be true: he would go and see the son he loved so much.

Jacob was one hundred and thirty years old when he travelled to Egypt with his family. Joseph came to meet his father. How they hugged one another and what a wonderful day it was for them both.

THINK AND PRAY: What a wonderful time for this family, all together once again. Thank God for joyful times when we see God's goodness and kindness to us. These might be: being well again after an illness; a birthday when we think of another year when God has been good to us; or Christmas time when we give thanks for the coming of the Lord Jesus.

DAY 12

God Speaks to Moses
Read: Exodus 3:9-10

There was a new Pharaoh in Egypt. He did not remember how Joseph had saved the Egyptians at the time of famine. Jacob's family grew very large as the years went by. They were called 'Israelites' after the new name God had given to Jacob.

The new Pharaoh did not like to see so many Israelites living in Egypt. He treated them very cruelly. They became slaves, building cities for the Egyptians. Pharaoh also tried to have all the little baby boys killed.

One baby boy, called Moses, was saved. His mother kept him hidden for three months. She then put him in a basket at the riverside. He was saved by Pharaoh's daughter. She brought him up as if he was her own son.

When Moses grew up, he wanted to help the Israelites, but they did not understand. He left

Egypt and settled down in the land of Midian. He lived in Midian for forty years.

One day, God spoke to Moses. God told him that He was going to bring the Israelites out of Egypt. Moses must go to Pharaoh and tell him to let the people go.

Moses thought of all sorts of reasons why he could not do as God said. He was not the right person, he could not speak very well, the people would not believe that God had sent him. God answered all that Moses said. At last Moses set out on the journey to Egypt.

It was not easy to tell Pharaoh 'God says, let my people go'. The Egyptians worshipped idols: they did not believe in the true God.

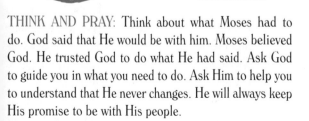

THINK AND PRAY: Think about what Moses had to do. God said that He would be with him. Moses believed God. He trusted God to do what He had said. Ask God to guide you in what you need to do. Ask Him to help you to understand that He never changes. He will always keep His promise to be with His people.

☀ DAY 13

Moses Leads the Israelites
Read: Exodus 14:21-22

Pharaoh did not want to let the Israelites go. They were useful to the Egyptians. They made bricks and did a lot of building for them.

God did many things in Egypt to show that He was the only true God. The Egyptians needed to learn that their idols were useless. The book of Exodus tells us all about what happened (Exodus chapters 8 to 13).

At last the Israelites were set free. They began their journey through the wilderness toward the land of Canaan. You might wonder how they knew the way. God sent a pillar of cloud ahead of them to show them the way. At night it became a pillar of fire to give them light.

God also spoke to Moses, telling him that the people must journey towards the Red Sea and camp there. God knew what was going to happen, but the Israelites did not know. They looked towards Egypt and saw Pharaoh and his army coming towards them. They seemed to be trapped between the Red Sea and Pharaoh's army. They cried out to God.

Moses told the people not to be afraid. They must stay where they were and God would save them. God moved the pillar of cloud so that it was between the Israelites and the Egyptians. Moses stretched out his hand holding his rod over the sea. God sent a strong wind all night. This divided the water. There was a dry path for the Israelites to go across. When they were all safely across the sea, God told Moses to stretch out his hand again. This time the water came back and the Egyptians were drowned.

The people thanked God for saving them from their cruel enemies.

THINK AND PRAY: The Israelites were afraid when they saw the Egyptian soldiers coming. What things frighten you or make you nervous? When we are afraid we can pray, and we know that God will hear our prayer.

DAY 14

Joshua, Moses' Helper
Read: Numbers 14:8-9

When Moses led the Israelites out of Egypt he was eighty years old. He needed a younger man to help him in the work God had given him to do. He chose a young man named Joshua.

Soon after the Israelites left Egypt, they were attacked by some people called Amalekites. Moses asked Joshua to choose some men to fight against them. Moses stood on a hill where the people could see him and held up his staff. Joshua and his men would know that Moses was praying that God would help them. They won the battle that day.

Joshua went with Moses, when God called him to come up the mountain where God spoke to him. He was learning a lot about what it was like to lead God's people.

When the Israelites came near to the land of Canaan, Moses chose twelve men to spy out the land. Joshua was one of them. They were to see what sort of land it was and what sort of people lived there.

After forty days travelling around Canaan, the twelve spies came back to where the Israelites were camped. They told them that Canaan was a good land for growing food. Then they said that the people of Canaan were very strong. They lived in large cities with high walls around them.

Ten of the spies made the Israelites feel very frightened. God had promised that the land of Canaan would be theirs. But how could they fight against the people the spies had told them about?

Only two spies believed that God was able to help them. They were Joshua and Caleb. You read some of what they said in today's Bible verses.

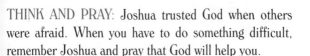

THINK AND PRAY: Joshua trusted God when others were afraid. When you have to do something difficult, remember Joshua and pray that God will help you.

☀ DAY 15

Joshua the Leader
Read: Joshua 1:1, 2 and 9

Joshua had been Moses' helper for forty years. The Israelites had lived in the wilderness ever since they refused to go into Canaan. They would not believe Joshua and Caleb who told them that God would help them to take the land as their own. God said they must stay in the wilderness for one year for each day the spies had been in Canaan: forty years.

Moses was one hundred and twenty years old, and his life was coming to an end. Moses asked God to put a new leader over the Israelites. God told him that the leader would be Joshua.

Joshua's task would begin by getting the many thousands of Israelites across the River Jordan. God caused the river to stop flowing and a way was made for the people to cross. Joshua made sure that the people understood that it was

God who had done this. God would also help them to fight against the people of Canaan.

The city of Jericho was near to where the Israelites had crossed the river. The people of Jericho were protected by high, strong walls and locked gates. God told Joshua exactly what to do. The people did as Joshua had told them and God caused the walls of the city to fall down.

All through his life Joshua trusted God and obeyed Him. He led the Israelites in many battles. Then he told them how to divide the land between them. He taught the people that if they obeyed God, He would be with them to help them.

Joshua lived to be one hundred and ten years old. Towards the end of his life he called the Israelites together. He spoke to them of all that God had done for them. The people promised that they would obey God.

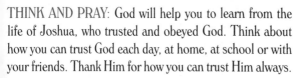

THINK AND PRAY: God will help you to learn from the life of Joshua, who trusted and obeyed God. Think about how you can trust God each day, at home, at school or with your friends. Thank Him for how you can trust Him always.

DAY 16

Caleb – Courageous and Calm
Read: Numbers 14:30;
Joshua 14:7-9

We have already learned that Caleb was one of the twelve spies that Moses sent into the land of Canaan. Ten of the spies made the Israelites afraid. They said the people in Canaan were too strong for the Israelites to fight against. Caleb tried to calm the people. He and Joshua told them that God would be with them. God would give them the land as He had promised.

The Israelites disobeyed God. God said that none of those who were over twenty years old at that time, except Caleb and Joshua, would ever live in their own land. It was forty years before God allowed the Israelites to enter Canaan, with Joshua as their leader.

The people of Israel were divided into twelve tribes, named after the twelve sons of Jacob.

Joshua and Eleazer the priest, divided the land between the tribes. By this time, Caleb was eighty-five years old. He asked Joshua to give him the land Moses had promised him.

Moses had made this promise when Caleb told the people to trust God to help them. Moses said that Caleb 'had wholly followed the Lord'. Caleb had seen the strong fighting men of Canaan. He had seen the high walls around the cities. He was not afraid, like ten of the spies, because he believed God. God had promised that He would give the land of Canaan to the Israelites. Caleb knew that God would do as He said.

Joshua gave Caleb the city of Hebron. Caleb was an old man now, but still trusting God to help him take over the city.

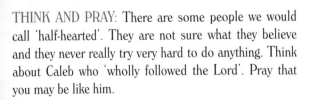

THINK AND PRAY: There are some people we would call 'half-hearted'. They are not sure what they believe and they never really try very hard to do anything. Think about Caleb who 'wholly followed the Lord'. Pray that you may be like him.

Day 17

Gideon Builds an Altar
Read: Judges 6:11-12

After Joshua died, the Israelites forgot all that God had done for them. They even began to worship idols like the Canaanites did. When this happened, God did not help them against their enemies. Life became very difficult for them.

When the Israelites remembered that they should trust God and obey Him, God helped them. He gave them leaders called 'Judges' who led them in battle against their enemies.

For seven years the Midianites made life hard for the Israelites. They destroyed the crops so that there was no food for the people. At last, the Israelites called on God to help them.

God heard their prayer. He sent a prophet to them. You will remember that a prophet is a person that God speaks to, so that he will give God's message to the people. This prophet reminded them of all that God had done for them. He told them that God had said they must not worship false gods. They had disobeyed God.

After this, an Angel spoke to a man named Gideon. He told Gideon that he was sending him to save the Israelites from the Midianites. Gideon wondered how he could do this, but the Angel promised that God would be with him. There was something that Gideon was told he must do before he could lead the people to battle.

Gideon's father had an altar where he made offerings to a false god called Baal. The Angel told Gideon that he must destroy this altar and build an altar to the true God. This was not easy for Gideon to do, but he took some men with him at night. They pulled down the altar and the idol that was beside it. Then they built an altar as the Angel had told them.

THINK AND PRAY: Think about how the people had to learn that idols are useless. They cannot help anyone. Only God hears our prayers and is able to help us. Give time out of each day to pray to God. He is the one true God.

✳ DAY 18

Gideon's Three Hundred Men
Read: Judges 7:2

Gideon called a lot of people to help him to fight against the Midianites. God told him that there were too many. He told Gideon to let all the men who were afraid go home. A lot of men went home. Ten thousand men stayed with Gideon.

God said that even ten thousand was still too many. He said that Gideon must take the men down to the stream to drink. Most of the men got down on their knees to drink from the stream. Just three hundred of them drank water that they held in their hands. God said that the three hundred were to go with Gideon.

Three hundred was not very many to fight against thousands of Midianites. God wanted the Israelites to know that He would save them from their enemies. They must trust in Him, not in having lots of soldiers.

Gideon gave each man a trumpet, a pot (called a pitcher) and a torch. (Their torches would have been wood set on fire.) Gideon divided his men into three groups of one hundred. He told them to watch him and do as he did. They came to the camp of the Midianites in the middle of the night.

Watching Gideon, all the men blew their trumpets and broke the pitchers that held their torches. They shouted, 'The sword of the Lord and of Gideon'. The sound of the trumpets and the lighted torches all around their camp, frightened the Midianites.

The Midianites began fighting each other and then ran away. Gideon then called more men to help him to go after them. The leaders of the Midianites were killed and their land taken over for the Israelites.

THINK AND PRAY: God was teaching the Israelites to trust Him to help them. Pray that God will help you to learn this lesson too.

DAY 19

Samuel – A Prayed-for Child
Read: 1 Samuel 3:10

Hannah had longed to have children to love and care for. She prayed that God would give her a little boy. She promised that if God did this, she would give her son to God. God heard Hannah's prayer. She had a baby boy and called him Samuel, which means 'heard by God'.

While Samuel was still very young, Hannah took him to the tabernacle. She left him with Eli the priest. Samuel was to be Eli's helper. The tabernacle was where the Israelites came to worship God. It was a special tent made by following instructions given to Moses by God. The Israelites carried it with them when they travelled through the wilderness. When they came into the land of Canaan, the tabernacle was set up in a city called Shiloh.

Samuel's family belonged to the tribe of Levi. God had chosen this tribe to help the priests at the tabernacle.

One night Samuel lay down to sleep. He heard someone call his name. He hurried to Eli, but Eli said he had not called him. Samuel went and lay down again. This happened twice. Then Samuel heard his name a third time. When he went to Eli again, Eli realised that it was God who was calling Samuel.

Eli told Samuel that if God called his name again, he must say, 'Speak Lord, for your servant hears'. Samuel did as Eli said, and God spoke to him about Eli and his sons.

Eli's sons were wicked men. It was hard for Samuel to tell Eli how displeased God was with them. Eli wanted to hear all that God had said. He understood that his sons deserved to be punished for their wrong doing.

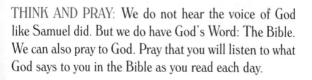

THINK AND PRAY: We do not hear the voice of God like Samuel did. But we do have God's Word: The Bible. We can also pray to God. Pray that you will listen to what God says to you in the Bible as you read each day.

DAY 20

Samuel the Judge
Read: 1 Samuel 3:19-20

When Samuel grew up he became the leader of the Israelites. He was the last of the Judges. The enemies of Israel at that time were the Philistines. Samuel taught the people not to bow down to the idols that other nations worshipped. If they trusted God, He would help them to fight against the Philistines. The people listened to Samuel and they were saved from their enemies.

Samuel served God and helped the Israelites all through his life. But when he was old, the people said that they wanted a king to rule over them. This made Samuel sad. He prayed to God about it. God said the people could have a king.

God told Samuel who was to be the king. His name was Saul and Samuel anointed him with oil. This was a way of showing that he had been chosen to be king of Israel.

King Saul began well, leading the people in battle against the Philistines. As time went by, he did not always obey God. Once again Samuel was very sad, but God said He would choose another man to be king after Saul.

God told Samuel to go to Bethlehem. There he was to see the family of a man named Jesse. God had chosen one of Jesse's sons to be the next king: Samuel must anoint him. Samuel thought of how angry Saul would be if he heard about this. Samuel would be putting himself in great danger. But he obeyed God and went to Bethlehem to meet Jesse's family.

THINK AND PRAY: God is in charge of all things – even the people who are in charge of you, like Kings and Presidents. Pray that you will learn to trust God while you are young, like Samuel did.

DAY 21

David the Shepherd
Read: 1 Samuel 17:45

David lived in Bethlehem. He was the youngest son of Jesse. One day, Samuel came to Bethlehem. He was going to offer a sacrifice to God. He invited Jesse and his sons to come with him. David was left at home to look after the sheep.

Samuel met David's seven older brothers. He knew that God had not chosen any of them to be the next king. At last David was sent for and God told Samuel that this was the one He had chosen. Samuel anointed David with oil.

It would be a long time before David would become King of Israel. He still looked after his father's sheep. His three older brothers had gone to help King Saul to fight against the Philistines.

One day, Jesse sent David to the place where the battle was. He gave David food to take to his brothers and the other soldiers.

Of cause, Jesse wanted to know how his three sons were getting on.

David found that the Israelite soldiers were afraid. A Philistine giant, Goliath, called every day for someone to come and fight him. David told King Saul that he would fight the giant. Saul thought that David was too young to be able to do this.

David told the King how God had helped him when the sheep were attacked by wild animals. He had killed a lion and a bear. David was sure that God would help him

to fight Goliath. David took his shepherd's staff, his sling and five smooth stones. David had learned to use his sling to protect the sheep. Now he used his sling to send a stone straight at the Philistine. The stone hit Goliath on the forehead. The giant fell to the ground.

THINK AND PRAY: Think about how David learned to trust God while he looked after the sheep. This was why he was not afraid of Goliath. Ask God to teach you how to trust in Him, and how to pray to Him.

DAY 22

David the King
Read: Psalm 23

King Saul was jealous of David, especially after David killed Goliath. For many years David had to move about the land of Israel so that Saul would not find him.

At last, when David was about thirty years old, King Saul died in a battle with the Philistines. The people in the South of Israel anointed David as their king. Seven years later, he became king over all Israel.

David was the greatest of all the kings of Israel. He was not perfect, but when he had done wrong, he was truly sorry for his sin. He knew that God had forgiven him.

David wanted to build a temple, in place of the tabernacle that had been used in the wilderness. God said 'no'. David had fought many battles. The temple would be built by his son in a quieter, more peaceful time. David showed that he really loved God by the way he tried to have everything ready for the temple. He collected as much as he could of things that would be needed: gold, silver, bronze, iron, wood and precious stones. He was disappointed that God said he should not build the temple, but he did everything he could to have things ready for his son, Solomon.

David also wrote many of the Psalms that we find in the Old Testament Book of Psalms. You read one of these today. You will remember that David had been a shepherd. He knew all about caring for the sheep. In Psalm 23, David tells us that God looks after His people, just as a good shepherd looks after his sheep.

David knew that all through his life, God had been his shepherd. God had led him in the right way.

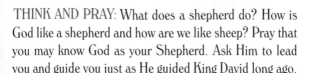

THINK AND PRAY: What does a shepherd do? How is God like a shepherd and how are we like sheep? Pray that you may know God as your Shepherd. Ask Him to lead you and guide you just as He guided King David long ago.

✳ DAY 23

Jonathan, the True Friend
Read: 1 Samuel 23:16

Jonathan's father was King Saul. Jonathan knew that he would not be king after his father. He knew that God had chosen David to be the next king. He was not jealous like his father. He became David's true friend.

Jonathan was brave. He even fought against some of the Philistines on his own. After David killed Goliath, Jonathan saw that he was brave as well. This was when they became friends. Jonathan spoke to his father about David, because he knew that Saul wanted to have David killed. He reminded Saul of how bravely David had fought against Goliath.

King Saul listened to Jonathan, but he did not change. David had to go away. King Saul sent men to search for him. There was a time when Jonathan knew where David was. He did not tell his father. He went to meet David and spoke to him as you read in today's Bible verse. Jonathan helped David to keep trusting in God.

Jonathan was a true friend to David, but he could not always be with him. He had to go wherever his father sent him. He wanted his father to treat David properly, but he could not change his father or stop him being jealous.

There is only one Friend who can always be with us: the Lord Jesus. He promised, to all those who trust in Him, 'I will never leave you or forsake you'. To forsake someone means to stop being their friend and leave them on their own. The Lord Jesus promised that He would never do that to any boy or girl or grown-up who loves and trusts Him.

THINK AND PRAY: Think about what it means to have a Friend who can be with you always. If we trust the Lord Jesus to be our Saviour who has forgiven our sins, we will know Him as our greatest Friend.

DAY 24

King Asa's Prayer
Read: 2 Chronicles 14:11

Asa was the great-great-grandson of King David. When Asa became king of Judah (the southern part of the land of Israel) some of the people were worshipping idols. King Asa had the idols destroyed. He taught the people that they should worship the true God and obey Him.

For some time there was peace in Judah. Then a large army of one million soldiers came to fight against Judah. King Asa had only about half as many soldiers in his army. He called on God for help. You read the words of his prayer in today's Bible verse. We learn from Asa's prayer that he trusted God to help his people. He knew that it would not matter who had the biggest army. God was able to help with a small army just as with a large one.

God heard Asa's prayer and his army won the battle. After the battle, God sent a message to King Asa by the prophet Azariah. He told the king to be strong and keep trusting in God. After this, Asa went on removing any idols from the land. He called the people together, and they made a promise to seek God with all their heart. Once again the land was peaceful.

The true story of King Asa has a warning for us. We have seen how he trusted God when a large army came against him. But later in his life, instead of trusting God, he sent silver and gold to the king of Syria. He wanted the king of Syria to help him. Once again God sent a prophet with a message to the king. God said that Asa had been foolish to trust the king of Syria instead of trusting Him. Asa was angry and had the prophet put in prison.

THINK AND PRAY: When Asa was told he had been foolish he did not say sorry or repent. What do we do when someone corrects us? When you pray today, ask God to help you to trust in Him all through your life and to repent of your sin..

☀ DAY 25

Jehoshaphat's Prayer
Read: 2 Chronicles 20:5-7

Asa's son Jehoshaphat became king of Judah after his father died. Jehoshaphat wanted to make sure that the people obeyed God. He sent priests and their helpers the Levites, to teach the people God's law.

Jehoshaphat became a rich and powerful king. The countries around Judah did not even try to fight against him for a long time.

After King David and his son Solomon were kings of Israel, the land was divided in two. The northern part was still called Israel. The southern part was called Judah. Both parts had their own king. None of the kings of Israel obeyed God.

When Jehoshaphat was king of Judah, the king of Israel was Ahab. Ahab married a woman called Jezebel who worshipped an idol called Baal. Ahab built a temple for Baal and worshipped the idol.

One day Jehoshaphat went to visit Ahab. Ahab asked him to go with him to fight the Syrians. Jehoshaphat said that he would go. He was almost killed in battle, but God helped him. King Ahab was wounded and died.

God sent the prophet Hanani to meet Jehoshaphat. He told him that he had been wrong to help King Ahab who did not love God. After that, Jehoshaphat did everything he could to make sure the people of Judah obeyed God's law.

A message came to Jehoshaphat that a great army was coming against Judah. The people of Judah gathered together and Jehoshaphat prayed. You read the beginning of his prayer in today's Bible verses. God sent a message to the people, telling them not to be afraid, The armies that had joined together to fight against Judah, began to fight each other. Many were killed. The people of Judah were kept safe.

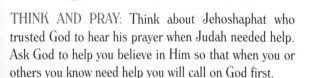

THINK AND PRAY: Think about Jehoshaphat who trusted God to hear his prayer when Judah needed help. Ask God to help you believe in Him so that when you or others you know need help you will call on God first.

DAY 26

An Uncle Hides a King
Read: 2 Chronicles 24:2

You will remember that Jehoshaphat was a good king in Judah while Ahab was a very bad king in Israel. Even people who love God sometimes do things that are not wise. Jehoshaphat arranged for his son to marry Athaliah the daughter of King Ahab. Athaliah brought the wicked ways of Israel into Judah.

Athaliah wanted to be the Queen in Judah so she did a terrible thing. She knew that one of her grandchildren should become king. She decided she would kill her own grandchildren.

Jehoiada the priest was the uncle of these royal children. His wife Jehosheba saw what was happening. She could not save them all but she did save little Joash who was just one year old.

Uncle Jehoiada and Aunty Jehosheba knew that they must keep Joash safe from the wicked queen. They hid him in the temple for six years.

What sad years those were for the people who really trusted in God. God had promised King David that there would always be a king from his family. Now it seemed that there was no king.

Jehoiada waited until Joash was seven years old. Then he decided that Joash must be crowned as king. He made sure there were enough people in the temple to protect him. Joash was crowned and that wicked Athaliah was put to death.

How could seven year old Joash know how to do all the things a king must do? As long as Uncle Jehoiada was alive, he helped the young king.

THINK AND PRAY: Jehoiada did what was right and was not afraid of what Queen Athaliah might do to him. Pray that God will always help you to do right and not be afraid.

DAY 27

The Prophet Elijah
Read: 1 Kings 17:14

Elijah was a prophet when Ahab was the king of Israel. The Bible tells us that Ahab was worse than any of the kings before him. You already know that he worshipped the false god, Baal. It was not easy for Elijah to give a message from God to such a wicked king.

Elijah had to tell Ahab that there would not be any rain for three years. This would mean that the crops would not grow. There would be a famine in the land. The people would soon be short of food.

God told Elijah to hide by a brook. God promised that the ravens would bring him food. He would be able to drink water from the brook. The ravens came with food in the morning and in the evening.

Because there was no rain, Elijah must have seen the water in the brook getting less each day.

At last the brook dried up altogether. God told Elijah to go to a place called Zarephath. There was a widow who would give him food. A widow is a lady whose husband had died. This widow was very poor. She had just enough food for one meal for her and her son. She thought that after that, they would die.

Elijah travelled to Zarephath and met the widow collecting sticks to make a fire to cook on. He asked her for some bread. She explained that she was just going to bake her very last loaf. Elijah told her to bring him some of her bread. He said that God would make sure that she had enough flour and enough oil, until He sent rain.

The widow did as Elijah said. Elijah stayed with her and there was always enough flour and oil to make bread for him and the widow and her son.

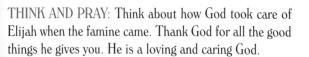

THINK AND PRAY: Think about how God took care of Elijah when the famine came. Thank God for all the good things he gives you. He is a loving and caring God.

✳ DAY 28

Elijah and the False Prophets
Read: 1 Kings 18:26-27

In the third year without rain, God sent Elijah to King Ahab again. Ahab had been searching for Elijah. He blamed him for bringing famine on the land. Elijah told the king that God had sent a famine because Ahab, and the kings before him, disobeyed God and worshipped idols.

Elijah said that Ahab must gather the people together at Mount Carmel. Elijah spoke to the people. He told them that it was time for them to make up their minds whether they would follow the true God or their idol, Baal. There were hundreds of false prophets there. Men who worshipped Baal and taught the people to do the same.

Elijah said that there must be a sacrifice on an altar for Baal, and another for the true God. The false prophets must call on Baal to send fire on the sacrifice. Elijah would then call on God. The people would see who would answer by sending fire.

The false prophets spent the whole morning calling on Baal. Elijah made fun of them, saying that Baal might be busy, or asleep or have gone on a long journey. Still Baal's prophets called on their false god all through the afternoon.

Then came evening time. Elijah called the people to him. Calmly, he prayed that God would let the people see that God heard him and would answer his prayer. Fire came down upon the sacrifice. The people bowed down. They had seen that their idol was of no use. Idols cannot hear or do anything in answer to prayer. Only God could send fire when Elijah prayed.

THINK AND PRAY: Elijah stood in front of all the people, and prayed. He trusted God to answer his prayer. When you pray today, thank God that He still hears and answers prayer.

DAY 29

Elisha and the Widow
Read: 2 Kings 4:2

In the Bible we read about two people who did not die: God took them to be with Himself. One was Enoch who we read about in Genesis chapter 5 verses 21 to 24, and Hebrews chapter 11 verse 5. The other was the prophet Elijah, who we have been learning about.

God sent another prophet called Elisha to the people of Israel. He had been a helper to Elijah.

One day a widow in great trouble came to see Elisha. She owed some money and could not pay it back. The man who she owed the money to, said that he would take the widow's two sons to be his slaves. This meant that they would have to leave their mother and work for him. Elisha asked the widow what she had in the house. She only had a pot of oil. He told her what she must do.

The widow did exactly what Elisha had told her to do. She borrowed lots of pots from her neighbours: anything that would hold oil. She closed the door. Her sons passed her the empty pots one by one. She filled each one by pouring oil from her own pot. The oil kept coming until all the pots were full. She told Elisha what had happened.

Elisha told the widow to sell the oil to pay back the money she owed. The money that was left would be enough for her and her two sons to buy food.

You might wonder how the widow's one pot of oil became enough to fill many pots. This was a miracle: something that only God could do. Elisha trusted God: he knew that God could do this. The miracles that happened at the time of the prophets, showed that God was with them and that the people must listen to their words.

THINK AND PRAY: The truths and miracles we read about in God's Word show us that we must also pay attention to what God is saying to us. Pray that God will speak to you as you read the Bible each day.

DAY 30

Elisha and Naaman
Read: 2 Kings 5:15

Naaman was a very important man in Syria. He was in charge of all the soldiers. He was a brave man, but he had an illness called leprosy. In those days there was no medicine to make him better.

Naaman's wife had a little servant girl. The soldiers had brought her from the land of Israel. She told Naaman's wife about Elisha the prophet. She was sure he would be able to make Naaman better. The king of Syria sent a letter to the king of Israel. He asked the king of Israel to make Naaman well again. The king knew that he could not do this. He was afraid the Syrians would be angry. Elisha heard all about it. He told the king to send Naaman to him.

Naaman came to Elisha's house. Elisha sent a message to him. Naaman must go to the River Jordan and wash seven times.

Naaman was not pleased. He thought that the rivers in Syria were better than the River Jordan. Why should he do such a thing when Elisha had not even spoken to him?

Naaman's servants persuaded him to do as the prophet said. He went to the river and dipped himself seven times in the water. When he came out of the water the seventh time, the leprosy had gone. Naaman was well again.

Naaman went back to Elisha's house to give him a present. Elisha would not take anything. He wanted Naaman to understand that it was God, not Elisha, who had made him well.

THINK AND PRAY: You read some of Naaman's words in today's Bible verse. He had learned that the God Elisha worshipped was the only true God. God does not always work a miracle to make people better. When you pray today, thank God that He gave us bodies that are able to heal. Thank Him too for doctors and nurses who help us when we are ill.

DAY 31

Nehemiah and the Wall
Read: Nehemiah 2:4-5

Nehemiah loved the city of Jerusalem where the temple was. He lived in Persia with a lot of other people from Judah. They had been taken away from their own land because the people of Judah had disobeyed God and had worshipped idols. Nehemiah loved and trusted God. He was very sad when he heard news from Jerusalem. He heard that the city wall was broken down. The city gates had been burned. Nehemiah prayed. He knew that if the people were truly sorry for their sins, God would help them.

Nehemiah was a servant of King Artaxerxes. The king asked why Nehemiah looked so sad. While Nehemiah was telling the king about Jerusalem, he was also praying to God. God heard his silent prayer. The king agreed to let Nehemiah go to Jerusalem.

Nehemiah did not tell many people why he had come to Jerusalem. First, he looked carefully at the walls and the gates, so that he would know what must be done.

Nehemiah called the people to come and build up the wall of the city. Many people came, ready to work. Some people in the land were enemies of the Jews. They did not want to see Jerusalem's walls rebuilt. They even said they would attack the builders.

Nehemiah heard about these plans. He put people in place with swords and spears to protect the work. Even those who were building carried swords. Nehemiah told the people not to be afraid. They must remember their great God.

Those who plotted against the Jews could not stop the work. The walls were soon finished and the gates were in place.

THINK AND PRAY: Nehemiah prayed and worked. He did not pray and hope that the work would be done somehow. He did not work without asking for God's help. Pray that you will be like Nehemiah and show that you trust in God by the things that you do.

DAY 32

Jeremiah the Prophet
Read: Jeremiah 1:6-8

The Bible is a very special book. This is because it was God who helped the men who wrote the Bible, to write the words He wants us to hear. In the days when no-one had the whole Bible like we do now, God sent prophets to take His message to the people.

Jeremiah knew that God had made him a prophet to the people of Judah. When he was young, he did not know how he could speak to the people. God promised that He would be with Jeremiah.

The task that God gave to Jeremiah was very difficult. The people were worshipping the idols that the people around Judah bowed down to. They had forgotten how good God had been to them. They did not want to hear Jeremiah's message.

Jeremiah had to tell the people that unless they were truly sorry for their sin, they would be taken away from their own land. Men who pretended to be prophets told the people not to listen to Jeremiah. They said that nothing bad would happen to them.

Jeremiah was put in prison, only because the king and the people did not want to hear the truth. One day, Jeremiah was put into a deep dungeon where he could have starved to death. He was saved by a brave man called Ebed Melech. Ebed Melech spoke to the king about Jeremiah and the king allowed him to rescue him.

Jeremiah was sad because he knew that the people took no notice of God's words. He had warned them many times what would happen to them. God is very patient, but at last many of the people of Judah were taken captive to the land of Babylon.

THINK AND PRAY: Think about Jeremiah, how he kept on trusting God and obeying Him, even though the people did not believe his words. Ask God to help you believe the words you read in His Word.

✳ DAY 33

Daniel's Diet
Read: Daniel 1:5

Everything that Jeremiah had warned the Jewish people about, happened. Nebuchadnezzar the King of Babylon, came with his soldiers against the land of Judah. Many people were taken captive and had to leave their own land.

Daniel was a clever, good looking young man. King Nebuchadnezzar wanted young men like Daniel to work for him. Daniel and his friends were taken to Babylon. They were to have three years to learn the language and everything that was taught in Babylon.

The Babylonians worshipped idols. Daniel made up his mind that he would obey God. This would not be easy away from his home and his own land.

The king wanted the young men to have good food and wine from his palace. God had given the Jewish people rules about their food. Daniel and his friends did not think it was right to eat the king's food. Daniel spoke to the man in charge of them. He asked for plain food and water to drink. The man in charge was afraid that Daniel and his three friends would not look as well as the other young men. However, he allowed them to try their plain food for ten days.

At the end of the ten days, Daniel and his friends looked better than the young men who had eaten the king's food. After this, Daniel and his friends were given the food they had asked for.

It may seem strange to us that Daniel was so anxious about eating the right food. But this tells us something about him.

Daniel loved God and wanted to please God in everything he did. He was not afraid of King Nebuchadnezzar. He trusted God to protect him.

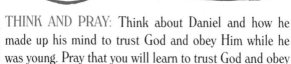

THINK AND PRAY: Think about Daniel and how he made up his mind to trust God and obey Him while he was young. Pray that you will learn to trust God and obey Him while you are young.

83

DAY 34

Daniel Keeps on Praying
Read: Daniel 6:7

After three years in Babylon, Daniel and his three friends were taken to the king. King Nebuchadnezzar soon found that there was no-one in Babylon as wise as these four young men.

As time went by, King Nebuchadnezzar made Daniel one of the three most important men in the land. Then he planned to put Daniel in charge of all the men who ruled over Babylon. The other men were not happy about that. They knew how honest Daniel was. They would not be able to cheat or do anything dishonest if Daniel was in charge.

These men tried to think of something that Daniel did wrong, so they could tell the king. They could not think of anything, so they made a plan. They knew that Daniel prayed to God. They asked the king to make a new law. For thirty days,

no-one must ask or pray for anything from anyone except the king. This would make the king feel very important indeed, so he agreed to the plan.

When Daniel heard about the new law, he did exactly what he always did. Three times every day, Daniel went to his room, knelt down, and prayed. Of course his enemies were watching and they soon told the king that Daniel had broken the law.

The king realised he had been tricked, but he could not change the law or the punishment. Daniel was put into the lions' den. The king could not sleep all night. Early in the morning he went to the den, and called to Daniel. How amazed he was when Daniel answered. Daniel told the king that God had sent His angel to shut the mouths of the lions, so that they could not harm him.

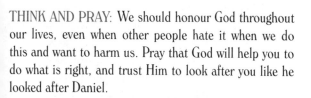

THINK AND PRAY: We should honour God throughout our lives, even when other people hate it when we do this and want to harm us. Pray that God will help you to do what is right, and trust Him to look after you like he looked after Daniel.

☀DAY 35

Zacharias and the Angel
Read: Luke 1:13

Zacharias the priest and his wife Elizabeth loved and obeyed God. They did not have children to care for and had prayed to God for a family. The years went by until they were older than parents usually are when a baby is born.

One day, when Zacharias was in the Temple, an angel appeared to him. Zacharias was afraid but the angel told him not to be afraid. The angel said that God had heard his prayers. Elizabeth would have a baby boy, who they must call John. The angel told Zacharias that when John grew up, he would have a special job to do. He would get the people ready for the Saviour God had promised to send.

Zacharias found it hard to believe what the angel had said because he and Elizabeth were getting old. The angel knew that as he had brought a message from God Zacharias should have believed him. So Zacharias was told that until the baby was born, he would not be able to speak.

Elizabeth did have a baby boy, just as the angel had said. When the baby was eight days old, it was time to give him his name. Elizabeth's friends and relations thought the baby would be called Zacharias after his father. Elizabeth said no, he was to be called John. They all looked at Zacharias to know what he thought. He wrote 'his name is John' and when he had done that, he was able to speak again.

Zacharias thanked God for keeping His promise to send a Saviour.

THINK AND PRAY: Zacharias understood the task that God was going to give John. He showed by his words that he really did trust God: he believed the Old Testament promises about the Saviour. When you pray today, ask God to help you to believe in Jesus, the promised Saviour.

DAY 36

Joseph the Husband of Mary
Read: Luke 2:7

Joseph and Mary lived in the city of Nazareth. They were engaged to be married. It should have been a very happy time, as they looked forward to their wedding day. But Joseph was puzzled and anxious. He knew that Mary was going to have a baby and they were not married yet. What should he do?

God knew all about Joseph. He sent an angel to appear to Joseph in a dream. The angel explained that Mary's Baby was very special. This Baby's Father was God Himself, because this Baby was the promised Saviour. He was to be given the name Jesus – a name that means 'Saviour'.

Joseph realised that he and Mary should get married, as they had planned. Then he would be able to look after Mary and the Baby.

Just at that time, the Roman Emperor said that everyone must go to the town their family first came from. This was so that everyone could be counted. Mary and Joseph had to travel to Bethlehem, where King David had lived long before. They belonged to the family of King David. They had a long way to travel, with no cars, buses, trains or aeroplanes. They might have had a donkey to ride on, or they might have had to walk all the way.

While Mary and Joseph were in Bethlehem, Jesus was born. There was no crib with warm blankets ready for Him. Mary and Joseph were far from home. The Baby Jesus was laid in a manger where the animals' food was usually placed.

THINK AND PRAY: Hundreds of years before Jesus was born, God spoke to Micah the prophet. He told Micah that the Saviour would be born in Bethlehem (Micah chapter 5 verse 2). The Roman Emperor did not know that he was helping to make this happen. When you pray today, thank God that what he has promised, always happens just as He has said.

DAY 37

Simeon in the Temple
Read: Luke 2:25-26

When we look at the sun, moon and the stars in the sky, we know that there must be a wonderful God who made them. When we watch all the different kinds of animals, and when we see the beautiful flowers and trees, we want to thank God for this amazing world. But there is something that stops us knowing God as our Friend. It is our sin: all the wrong things we do, say or think, because we have sinful hearts.

We have learned that God had promised to send Someone who would save us from our sin. He would do this by living a perfect life and then dying to take the punishment we deserve. This is what the Lord Jesus did for everyone who trusts in Him.

About two thousand years ago, in Jerusalem, there were some people who believed God's promises and were longing for the Saviour to come. One of those people was a man named Simeon. God had given Simeon a special promise that before he died, he would see the Saviour.

One day, Simeon knew that God was telling him to go to the temple. When he got there, he saw a man and woman with a baby. It was Mary and Joseph bringing the Baby Jesus to the temple. God had taught His people to do this after a baby had been born. Simeon took the Baby in his arms and thanked God for Him. Joseph and Mary were amazed at the words he spoke. Simeon knew that this Baby was the promised Saviour.

All that we know about Simeon is in Luke's Gospel chapter 2. We do not know anything else about his life. We remember him as someone who loved God and trusted in God's promise.

THINK AND PRAY: Think about Simeon who was waiting to see the Saviour. Pray that you will trust in Jesus as Simeon did; that you will know He is the one and only Saviour.

DAY 38

Joseph Obeys God
Read: Matthew 2:1-2

After the Lord Jesus was born, Mary and Joseph stayed in Bethlehem for a while. One day they had some visitors from another land. These were the wise men we read about in Matthew chapter 2. Somehow these men knew that the star they saw meant that a new king had been born in the land of Israel.

The wise men went first to Jerusalem where King Herod lived. King Herod was not pleased. He did not want this special King who the wise men were looking for. He sent them to Bethlehem. They saw the star that they had seen in their own land. The star led them to the house where Mary and Joseph were staying.

The wise men bowed down to the Baby Jesus and gave Him gifts. God told them not to go back to tell King Herod where Jesus was. Herod was angry. He wanted to destroy this special Child.

An angel appeared to Joseph in a dream. He told Joseph to take Mary and the Lord Jesus, to the land of Egypt. There they would be safe from the king. Joseph got up in the night and took Mary and the Child Jesus to Egypt. This was an even longer journey for them to make than when they had travelled to Bethlehem.

They may not have had to stay in Egypt very long, because King Herod died. God told Joseph, in a dream, that it would be safe now for them to go back to their home. This would be their longest journey, all the way back to Nazareth.

THINK AND PRAY: Each time Joseph was told what to do, he was quick to obey. He did not spend time thinking about how tiring the journeys would be. He obeyed God because he trusted God. Pray that you may show your trust in God by doing what He says in the Bible.

DAY 39

John the Baptist
Read: Matthew 3:1-3

We have already learned about Zacharias and Elizabeth's baby, who was called John. Today we will learn, why, when he grew up, he was called 'John the Baptist'.

God gave many promises in Old Testament days, about the Lord Jesus coming into the world. He also promised that there would be someone to prepare the people for His coming. We read about this in the Book of Isaiah and the Book of Malachi.

We do not know how old John was when he understood that he was the one God had chosen for this task. We do know that when he began to speak to the people, he knew exactly what God wanted him to do.

Today's Bible verses tell us that John told the people they must repent. The word 'repent' means change from doing wrong things, to doing right things. It means more than just being sorry for our sin. You might be sorry if you had told a lie. If you repent, you will not just be sorry, you will stop telling lies.

Many people heard John speak and they came to him to be baptized in the River Jordan. Of course, water could not wash their sins away. But being baptised showed that they were sorry for their sins and wanted to change. It showed that they believed that God had the power to change them.

John also spoke to the people about the Lord Jesus. God had told John that Jesus was the promised Saviour. John called Jesus 'the Lamb of God'. You will remember that in Old Testament days, a lamb would die instead of someone who had done wrong. John understood that that was like a picture of what the Lord Jesus would do.

THINK AND PRAY: Think about John who trusted God and did the job God gave him to do. What does God want you to do today and how can you honour Him in those tasks? Pray that your life will show others how good God is.

DAY 40

Peter Follows Jesus
Read: Mark 1:16-17

Peter was a fisherman. He lived near to the Sea of Galilee. Peter's brother, Andrew, was with John the Baptist when John pointed to the Lord Jesus. Andrew believed that Jesus was the promised Saviour. He brought Peter to meet Jesus.

Peter and Andrew were chosen by Jesus to be His disciples. Many people came to listen to the Lord Jesus. But He chose twelve men to be with Him. They would hear all He said and see the wonderful things He did. Then they would be able to tell other people about Him.

Three days after the Lord Jesus died on the cross, He rose from the dead. We call this the resurrection. Soon He would go back to His Father in heaven. Before He left His disciples, He told them that they must be His witnesses. A witness is someone who can tell others what he has seen and heard. The disciples were to tell others about the Lord Jesus, especially about His death on the cross and His resurrection.

One day Peter was sent for by a Roman soldier called Cornelius. Until then, Peter had thought of his people the Jews, as very special. But God helped Peter to understand that everyone needed to hear about the Lord Jesus. He set off with the men Cornelius had sent to find him.

Cornelius had his family and his friends all ready to hear what Peter had to say. As Peter spoke about Jesus, Cornelius and all the people with him, believed.

As soon as Peter understood that he should tell people from different lands about the Lord Jesus, he obeyed God.

THINK AND PRAY: Pray that God will help you to tell people about Jesus. Even while you are very young, could you invite a friend to Sunday School or a children's meeting?

DAY 41

Andrew, the Bringer
Read: John 6:8-11

Andrew was a disciple of John the Baptist. As John told the people to be ready to meet the Saviour, Andrew was there. He listened to John's teaching. One day he heard John say, 'Look, the Lamb of God'. John was pointing to the Lord Jesus, as he said this.

Andrew would have understood what that meant. Every morning and every evening in the temple, a lamb died for the sins of the people. Calling Jesus the Lamb of God, meant that He would save people from their sins.

After listening to John the Baptist, Andrew was sure that Jesus was the Saviour who God had promised. He went to find Peter and told him this good news. Then he brought Peter to Jesus.

As we have already learned, both brothers were chosen by the Lord Jesus, to be His disciples.

In the New Testament we read more about Peter than about Andrew. But we do read about the times when Andrew brought someone to Jesus.

You may have heard the story that we usually call 'The feeding of the five thousand'. A great crowd of people had followed the Lord Jesus and He told the disciples they must give the people something to eat. Among all that great crowd, it was Andrew who found a boy with some food and brought him to Jesus. The boy only had five little loaves and two small fish. The Lord Jesus took the food and made a meal for thousands of people with it. This was a miracle that only God could do.

One day, Philip, one of the disciples, told Andrew that some men were asking to see Jesus. It seemed that Andrew would know what to do. He and Philip told Jesus about the men.

THINK AND PRAY: Andrew knew how to bring others to the Lord Jesus and how to tell the Lord Jesus about others. Ask God to teach you how to teach others about Himself.

DAY 42

John the Disciple
Read: John 3:16

Like Peter and Andrew, John and his brother James were fishermen. One day, when they were mending their fishing nets by the Sea of Galilee, Jesus called them to follow Him. They left their father in the boat and followed Jesus. They too became His disciples.

Like the other disciples, John was with Jesus for about three years. He listened to all that Jesus had to teach His disciples. He saw the wonderful miracles Jesus did, healing many people who were ill or blind or unable to walk.

When the Lord Jesus was arrested in order to be crucified (put to death on the cross) the disciples were very frightened. They were afraid to stay with Him in case something bad happened to them as well. But John did stay, and Jesus spoke to him from the cross. Jesus asked John to care for His mother, Mary.

John probably had a long life and lived to be an old man. At that time Christians were often punished for teaching people about the Lord Jesus. John was sent to an island called Patmos. The Lord Jesus spoke to him there from heaven. He told John to write what he saw and also the words he heard. We have what John wrote, in the last book of the Bible: the Book of Revelation.

John wrote four other New Testament books: John's Gospel and three letters to help Christians. John loved the Lord Jesus and wanted others to love Him too.

THINK AND PRAY: The words of today's Bible verse were spoken by the Lord Jesus and written down for us by John. This would be a good verse for you to learn: ask a grown up to help you. When you pray today, thank God that He loved us so much, that He sent His Son to die for us.

Day 43

Zaccheus the Tax Collector
Read: Luke 19:8-10

Zaccheus was a rich man, but he probably did not have many friends. People did not like tax collectors because they cheated. They collected money for the Roman Emperor to use for roads and buildings and soldiers. However, the people knew that tax collectors took too much money, and kept some for themselves.

One day, Zaccheus heard that Jesus was in town. He wanted to see Jesus, but he could not see because he was not tall enough. You may have been in a crowd where everyone was bigger than you. Unless someone lifts you up you just cannot see. There was no-one to lift Zaccheus up, but he had an idea.

Zaccheus hurried ahead of the crowd to a sycamore tree. He climbed the tree and had a good view of the road Jesus would come along. Zaccheus had a surprise. Instead of walking past the tree, Jesus stopped and looked up at him. He told Zacchaeus to hurry down, because He was coming to his house.

Zacchaeus did hurry. He was so happy that the Lord Jesus was coming to his house. Other people who were there were not happy. They said that Jesus had chosen to visit a man who was a sinner. Zacchaeus told the Lord Jesus that he would give half his money to the poor. He also said that he would give four times as much money as he had taken from people by cheating.

The Lord Jesus knew all about what people thought of Zacchaeus. He said that Zacchaeus was just the sort of person He had come to save.

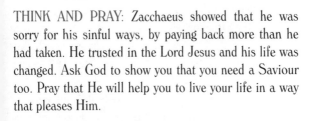

THINK AND PRAY: Zacchaeus showed that he was sorry for his sinful ways, by paying back more than he had taken. He trusted in the Lord Jesus and his life was changed. Ask God to show you that you need a Saviour too. Pray that He will help you to live your life in a way that pleases Him.

DAY 44

Stephen Sees Jesus
Read: Acts 7:59-60

After the Lord Jesus went back to heaven, the disciples did as He had told them. They spoke to the people about who Jesus was and what He had done. Many people became Christians: they trusted in the Lord Jesus to forgive their sin. They began to obey Him instead of pleasing themselves.

Some of the Christians were poor, especially those who were widows. The disciples began to help the widows, making sure that they had enough food to eat each day. This began to take up so much time that the disciples were not free to teach the people about the Lord Jesus. They called the Christians together. They asked them to choose seven men who would take care of the poor. Stephen was one of the seven men who were chosen.

Many of the Jewish people did not want to hear about the Lord Jesus. They began arguing with Stephen, but God helped him to answer everything they said. Some people told lies about him and he was taken to the priests and leaders of the people.

Stephen was not afraid. He talked to the leaders about things that had happened in the Old Testament days. How the Jewish people would not listen to the prophets God had sent. Then he told them that they had killed God's own Son, Jesus.

The men were very angry with Stephen, but still he was not afraid. He looked up and saw the Lord Jesus in heaven. The men picked up stones and used them to kill Stephen. As he was being stoned, he asked God not to blame the men for what they were doing.

THINK AND PRAY: Stephen was the first Christian to be put to death for speaking about Jesus. When you pray today, thank God for Christians who were not afraid to die, so that people like us could hear about the Lord Jesus.

☀DAY 45

Saul the Persecutor
Read: Acts 9:4-5

To persecute someone means to treat them very badly, even being very cruel to them.

Saul was a Pharisee. The Pharisees were men who wanted to keep God's law (the rules God made). They also added laws of their own. They believed that they were good people and that God would be pleased with them.

However, Saul hated Christians. He did not believe that Jesus was the Son of God. He made up his mind to try to stop Christians telling people about the Lord Jesus. He got permission to take Christians from the city of Damascus. He would bring them to Jerusalem to be punished.

Saul took some men with him and set off on the road to Damascus. Just when he was nearly there, a light, brighter than the sun, shone around him. Paul fell to the ground. Then he heard a voice. The voice was the Lord Jesus Christ. You read the words he heard in today's Bible verses.

Saul had been persecuting Christians. The Lord Jesus loved those who trusted in Him so much, that to hurt them was to hurt Him. Saul, the proud Pharisee, was trembling. He asked the Lord Jesus what he must do. He was told to go into Damascus and there he would be told what to do.

When Saul stood up, he found that he could not see. The men who were with him had to take his hand and lead him into the city. For three days Saul could not see and he did not eat or drink. Then God sent a man named Ananias to him. As Ananias spoke to him, Saul's sight came back. He was baptised to show that he had become a Christian.

Tomorrow we will learn about how Saul's life was changed, after the Lord Jesus spoke to him.

THINK AND PRAY: Find out about countries in the world where you are not allowed to read the Bible or worship Jesus. Pray to God for the Christians who live there. Then thank God that He is still changing the lives of people who trust in Him.

DAY 46

Paul the Missionary
Read: Acts 13:2

The Jewish people met in buildings called synagogues, to learn from the Old Testament. Saul began visiting the synagogues to teach the people about the Lord Jesus. People knew that Saul had persecuted Christians. They were amazed that he was now telling them that Jesus is the Son of God, as the Christians believed.

It was hard for the Christians in Jerusalem to believe that Saul had really changed. They were a little afraid of him. One of them, called Barnabas trusted Paul and took him to the church at Antioch. Saul stayed in Antioch for about a year. Then the church understood that God had chosen Saul and Barnabas to be missionaries. They would travel to many places, telling people about Jesus.

Saul is a Jewish name. When Saul began meeting many people who were not Jewish, he used the name Paul.

Wherever Paul and Barnabas went, some people became Christians. Other people became angry and did not want to hear about the Lord Jesus. Sometimes Paul was put in prison, sometimes he was badly hurt.

We often talk about church as if a church is a building. In the New Testament, the word church always means a group of people who have become Christians. Churches grew in the places Paul visited. He wanted to help them, but he knew he must keep travelling to other places. There were always more people who had not yet heard about the Lord Jesus. So Paul wrote letters, some to be read to whole churches, some to Christians who worked with him. These letters are in our Bible and still help Christians today.

THINK AND PRAY: You do not have to travel as many miles as Paul did, to be a missionary. Pray that as you grow up you will be a missionary, telling people about the Lord Jesus, wherever you are.

DAY 47

The Jailer Who Became a Christian
Read: Acts 16:29-31

Yesterday we learnt about Paul and Barnabas. Sometimes Paul travelled with Barnabas, sometimes with other Christians. He travelled to Philippi with three friends: Silas, Timothy and Luke. (Philippi was in the country now called Greece.)

Some men in Philippi became very angry with Paul and Silas. They told lies about them and Paul and Silas were beaten and then put into prison. Their legs were fastened so that they could not move about. It was very uncomfortable, and yet in the middle of the night Paul and Silas prayed and sang hymns. The other prisoners were listening to them. In the darkness, the prisoners felt the prison shaking. It was an earthquake. All the doors came open and the chains fell off the prisoners. The jailer woke up and saw what had happened. He thought that all the prisoners had escaped. If they had, he would be punished. He decided it would be better if he killed himself.

Paul called the jailer. He told him not to harm himself as all the prisoners were still there.

You read the verses that tell us what happened next. The jailer must have seen how different Paul and Silas were from the other prisoners. He wanted to know how he could be saved from sin: how he could become a Christian.

Paul and Silas talked to the jailer and he believed what they said. He put his trust in the Lord Jesus. We know that the jailer changed. He no longer treated Paul and Silas roughly. He washed their sores where they had been beaten. He took them to his house for a meal.

THINK AND PRAY: We have read about prophets and kings who trusted God. But it's not just powerful people we read about in the Bible. When you pray today thank God that a tax collector like Zacchaeus and a rough jailer, also put their trust in the Lord Jesus.

✳ DAY 48

Timothy, Paul's helper
Read: 2 Timothy 3:14-15

We read about Timothy's mother and grandmother, in Paul's second letter to Timothy. His mother's name was Eunice and his grandmother's name was Lois. They were both Christians. They taught Timothy from the Bible while he was very young. Of course at that time, the Bible was just the Old Testament. The New Testament had not yet been written. The Old Testament tells us about the time before Jesus was born in Bethlehem.

Timothy would have learned about God's promise to send Someone into the world who would be the Saviour. His mother and his grandmother may have told him that the One God had promised, had come, and that He was the Lord Jesus.

Paul said that since he was a child, Timothy had known what the Bible teaches. He understood that he needed to trust in the Lord Jesus.

We do not know how old Timothy was when he became a Christian. It may have been when Paul first came to Lystra, where Timothy lived. When Paul came to Lystra the second time, he asked Timothy to join with him and Silas in their travels.

Some people think that Timothy was not a very brave person. But he did trust God and he did travel to many places to tell people about the Lord Jesus. Sometimes Paul asked Timothy to stay for a while in places where the Christians needed someone to teach them. There are two letters in the New Testament, that Paul wrote to help Timothy.

THINK AND PRAY: All that Timothy learned from the Bible while he was young, helped him to understand that he needed the Lord Jesus to be his Saviour. When you pray today, ask God to help you to learn from the Bible while you are young, like Timothy did.

DAY 49

John Mark Turns Back
Read: 2 Timothy 4:11

John Mark's mother was called Mary. We know that she was a Christian. We read in the Book of Acts about Christians meeting at her house to pray together.

In the New Testament, 'John Mark' is often just called 'Mark'. He was a cousin of Barnabas. When Paul and Barnabas were setting out on their travels, they decided to take Mark with them. He was a young man and could be a great help to them.

The three men sailed to the island of Cyprus. They spoke to people there about the Lord Jesus. From Cyprus they sailed to a place called Perga in the country we know as Turkey. Mark left Paul and Barnabas there and he went back to his home in Jerusalem.

We do not know why Mark went home. We do know that travelling was very hard in those days.

It would also be difficult finding somewhere to stay in places the missionaries visited. After all their travelling, they found that people did not always want to hear about the Lord Jesus.

Whatever the reason was, Paul was sorry that Mark had left. The next time he was going to set off on a journey with Barnabas, Paul would not allow Mark to come. Barnabas took Mark with him to Cyprus and Paul chose a man named Silas to go with him.

It is good to know that later on Mark did become a useful worker. We know this because Paul asked Timothy to bring Mark to him, because Mark would be useful.

There are four books in the New Testament which tell us about the life of the Lord Jesus. One of those books was written by Mark.

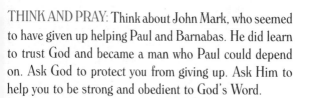

THINK AND PRAY: Think about John Mark, who seemed to have given up helping Paul and Barnabas. He did learn to trust God and became a man who Paul could depend on. Ask God to protect you from giving up. Ask Him to help you to be strong and obedient to God's Word.

DAY 50

Doctor Luke
Read: Acts 27:41, and 28:1-2

Luke wrote two of the books of the New Testament: the Gospel of Luke and the Acts of the Apostles. He was not a Jewish man like the other three Gospel writers, Matthew, Mark and John. He was trained as a doctor and he sometimes joined Paul in his travels.

Luke did not write about himself. But when he wrote in the Book of Acts about Paul and his helpers, he sometimes puts 'we' instead of 'they'. Whenever Luke puts 'we', we know that at that time he was with Paul.

Acts chapter 27 tells an amazing story of what it could be like to travel by sea in New Testament days. Paul was being taken to Rome as a prisoner. He had not done anything wrong, but people had told lies about him. He had been in prison in the land of Israel for quite a long time. Now he was being taken to the most important city in the empire. Luke was with Paul on the long journey across the Mediterranean Sea. They were ship-wrecked near the island of Malta. They had to stay there for three months before they could finish their journey.

Luke was a very faithful helper to Paul: Paul could rely on him. Once when Paul was writing a letter from prison, he said that Luke was the only person with him. In another letter, he writes of Luke as 'the beloved physician' (physician is another word for doctor).

We know that Luke was a man who loved, trusted and obeyed God. We know this from his life.

THINK AND PRAY: Luke faced the dangers of travelling in those days, so that others could hear about the Lord Jesus. He was there to help Paul even when he was in prison. Pray that you may grow up to show your love for the Lord Jesus by the way you live, as Luke did.

By the same Author

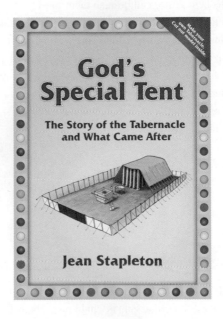

Make your own tabernacle. Cut out model inside.

God's Special Tent

The Story of the Tabernacle
and What Came After

Jean Stapleton

ISBN: 978-1-84550-811-1

Do you like tents? Perhaps you've gone camping, staying in one place and then moving to another. God's people the Israelites lived in tents in the wilderness as they moved from Egypt to the Promised Land. God gave them instructions about how to make a special tent – where He could be present among His people. Find out about how they made this tent and what special furniture and curtains were placed inside it. How did they build the tent and how did they carry it from one place to another? The priests made sacrifices to atone for the sin of the people, but the tabernacle or tent of meeting was a place that taught the people about the one who was going to save them from their sin for good – Jesus Christ, the promised Messiah. His sacrifice would mean that no other sacrifices were needed and that people could worship God all around the world.

By the same Author

Read with me

365 Family Readings Giving
An Overview Of The Bible

Jean Stapleton

ISBN: 978-1-84550-148-8

Read with Me takes the stories and teachings of the Bible from the beginning of the Old Testament through to the end of the New, explaining them in simple, direct language.

These devotions are ideal for reading to children – each one bringing out truths and questions, answers and lessons - and will bring your family closer to God.

For older family members there is an additional feature where, throughout the book, introductions are given to those Old and New Testament books that are featured. These give useful information for older children – or for adults to read alongside the family devotions.

This book is simple effective way to encourage your family to come together and spend time in a daily walk with God through his Word.

CHRISTIAN FOCUS PUBLICATIONS

Christian Focus | Christian Heritage | CF4K | Mentor

Christian Focus Publications publishes books for adults and children under its four main imprints: Christian Focus, CF4K, Mentor and Christian Heritage. Our books reflect our conviction that God's Word is reliable and Jesus is the way to know him, and live for ever with him.

Our children's publication list includes a Sunday School curriculum that covers pre-school to early teens, and puzzle and activity books. We also publish personal and family devotional titles, biographies and inspirational stories that children will love.

If you are looking for quality Bible teaching for children then we have an excellent range of Bible stories and age-specific theological books.

From pre-school board books to teenage apologetics, we have it covered!

Find us at our web page:
www.christianfocus.com

CF4•K
Because you're never
too young to know Jesus